Published by Angelis Publications
ISBN: 978-1-912484-11-9
www.angelispublications.com
© Angelis Publications 2018

A Celebration of the Life of

The tide recedes, but leaves behind
bright seashells on the sand.
The sun goes down, but gentle warmth
still lingers on the land.
The music stops, yet echoes on
in sweet, soulful refrains.
For every joy that passes
something beautiful remains.

Name & Address

Thoughts & Memories

Name & Address

Thoughts & Memories

Name & Address

Thoughts & Memories

Name & Address

Thoughts & Memories

Name & Address

Thoughts & Memories

Name & Address

Thoughts & Memories

Name & Address

Thoughts & Memories

Name & Address

Thoughts & Memories

Name & Address

Thoughts & Memories

Name & Address

Thoughts & Memories

Name & Address

Thoughts & Memories

Name & Address

Thoughts & Memories

Name & Address

Thoughts & Memories

Name & Address

Thoughts & Memories

Name & Address

Thoughts & Memories

Name & Address

Thoughts & Memories

Name & Address

Thoughts & Memories

Name & Address

Thoughts & Memories

Name & Address

Thoughts & Memories

Name & Address

Thoughts & Memories

Name & Address

Thoughts & Memories

Name & Address

Thoughts & Memories

Name & Address

Thoughts & Memories

Name & Address

Thoughts & Memories

Name & Address

Thoughts & Memories

Name & Address

Thoughts & Memories

Name & Address

Thoughts & Memories

Name & Address

Thoughts & Memories

Name & Address

Thoughts & Memories

Name & Address

Thoughts & Memories

Name & Address

Thoughts & Memories

Name & Address

Thoughts & Memories

Name & Address

Thoughts & Memories

Name & Address

Thoughts & Memories

Name & Address

Thoughts & Memories

Name & Address

Thoughts & Memories

Name & Address

Thoughts & Memories

Name & Address

Thoughts & Memories

Name & Address

Thoughts & Memories

Name & Address

Thoughts & Memories

Name & Address

Thoughts & Memories

Name & Address

Thoughts & Memories

Name & Address

Thoughts & Memories

Name & Address

Thoughts & Memories

Name & Address

Thoughts & Memories

Name & Address

Thoughts & Memories

Name & Address

Thoughts & Memories

Name & Address

Thoughts & Memories

Name & Address

Thoughts & Memories

Name & Address

Thoughts & Memories

Name & Address

Thoughts & Memories

Name & Address

Thoughts & Memories

Name & Address

Thoughts & Memories

Name & Address

Thoughts & Memories

Name & Address

Thoughts & Memories

Name & Address

Thoughts & Memories

Name & Address

Thoughts & Memories

Name & Address

Thoughts & Memories

Name & Address

Thoughts & Memories

Name & Address

Thoughts & Memories

Name & Address

Thoughts & Memories

Name & Address

Thoughts & Memories

Name & Address

Thoughts & Memories

Name & Address

Thoughts & Memories

Name & Address

Thoughts & Memories

Name & Address

Thoughts & Memories

Name & Address

Thoughts & Memories

Name & Address

Thoughts & Memories

Name & Address

Thoughts & Memories

Name & Address

Thoughts & Memories

Name & Address

Thoughts & Memories

Name & Address

Thoughts & Memories

Name & Address

Thoughts & Memories

Name & Address

Thoughts & Memories

Name & Address

Thoughts & Memories

Name & Address

Thoughts & Memories

Name & Address

Thoughts & Memories

Name & Address

Thoughts & Memories

Name & Address

Thoughts & Memories

Name & Address

Thoughts & Memories

Name & Address

Thoughts & Memories

Name & Address

Thoughts & Memories

Name & Address

Thoughts & Memories

Name & Address

Thoughts & Memories

Name & Address

Thoughts & Memories

Name & Address

Thoughts & Memories

Name & Address

Thoughts & Memories

Name & Address

Thoughts & Memories

Name & Address

Thoughts & Memories

Name & Address

Thoughts & Memories

Name & Address

Thoughts & Memories

Name & Address

Thoughts & Memories

Name & Address

Thoughts & Memories

CPSIA information can be obtained
at www.ICGtesting.com
Printed in the USA
LVHW101001040319
609386LV00026BA/654/P